Odes & *Laments*

Caitlin Press Inc.
8100 Alderwood Road,
Halfmoon Bay, BC V0N 1Y1
www.caitlin-press.com

Cover design by Vici Johnstone
Cover photo by Janet Little Jeffers
Illustrations by Taisia Aultman
Text design by Monica Miller
Printed in Canada

Caitlin Press Inc. acknowledges financial support from the Government of
Canada and the Canada Council for the Arts, and the Province of British
Columbia through the British Columbia Arts Council and the Book
Publisher's Tax Credit.

Library and Archives Canada Cataloguing in Publication

Title: Odes & Laments / Fiona Tinwei Lam.
Other titles: Odes and Laments
Names: Lam, Fiona Tinwei, 1964– author.
Description: Poems. | Includes bibliographical references.
Identifiers: Canadiana 20190117583 | ISBN 9781773860152 (softcover)
Classification: LCC PS8573.A38383 O34 2019 | DDC C811/.6—dc23

Odes & Laments

poems

Fiona Tinwei Lam

CAITLIN PRESS

Dedicated to Robbie and Ted

"A poetry of loam, where water can sing.
A poetry of bread, where everyone may eat."

—Pablo Neruda

CONTENTS

I

Libation

For me, no wine. Just the life's blood
of apples mashed whole
in a democracy of pulp—
skin, core, seeds, flesh,
warty or warped, bruised or scabbed,
joined to make juice
as round and real as Earth.
Let's open our tongues
to bitter soil, sweet scorch of sun,
crisp of autumn leaves,
shimmer of river. Forget
those tortured espaliered trees,
slaves chained to their stakes, forced
to sing their single notes.
Give us the old orchard's choir
of venerable trees, gnarled arms
held wide and high as tapers
knobbed with a decade's dripping wax.
Quaff the murky golden madrigals
of juice and know—all
revealed in a moment's swallow.
For what is juice but poetry?
What we've lived and known wrung out
of roots, trunk, guts, limbs
into the radiant fruit of now, seasoned
by wind and night. What's held within
this cup, this poem, this juice
I offer you.

Vision

Sting of dilation.
Past cornea, past iris,
through pupil, through
lens to retina, glowing
vermilion orb in the night
of the ophthalmologist's screen.
Flare of optic disk. Well of macula,
pit of fovea. Intricate mosaics
deciphering light.

No drusen yet, no golden portents
of waning vision that flecked
my mother's eyes. No signs
of war's twisting shadows
that sieved and warped our world
into sinister landscapes concealing
peril.

A decade after her death, a flash—
sudden dimness.
Behind my pupils, wisps
of torn vitreous dangle, tattered gauze.
    But beyond
her eyes or mine
is the vision
I need now
    to take me
    high, deep, far.

Let words
be my telescope
to enter the spiral whorls
of astral ancestors in deep space
or in fingertips, microscope

to travel the delicate labyrinths
of cells. Or magnifying glass—
the simplest lens
I can hold
close to petal, pebble,
leaf, flake, truth.

Plate

From Old French *plate* "thin piece of metal" (late 12c.),
from Medieval Latin *plata* "plate, piece of metal," perhaps
via Vulgar Latin *plattus*, formed on model of Greek *platys*
"flat, broad" (from PIE root "plat" to spread).
—"Plate," *Online Etymology Dictionary*

In ancient times, a domestic discus hurled
to smash death's cycle at funeral feasts.
Each crash, a shout of praise
for dancer, singer, bride and groom.

In Beijing, acrobats finesse
quivering blurs of balance
atop poles of bamboo. Moon
after moon restored to the heavens.

But it's mostly in cupboards we discover
you, stacked with your companions,
like fossilized vertebrae
of some squat prehistoric animal;
at intervals individuated,
buttoning down tables
during each day's plateaus.

Open palmed, you are expectant.
Sometimes, platforms
for buffet avalanches, converging
rivers of gravy, syrup, sauce and cream.
Other times in long wait, bereft,
yearning to flee Earth's despairs
like a B movie UFO.

But no longer.
Now, a shared pot, and here
are our portions: yours, mine,
encircled. Let abundance come
round with its daily embrace.

Chopsticks

Grandfather sets down the bowl full of marbles.
I pick up the chopsticks and hover,
then picture my hand as a heron
with a long, long beak plunging down
to pluck each orb, lift it
through air and held breath
in a tremulous trip toward the saucer.

Five thousand years of evolution in hand:
branches honed to stir ancient cauldrons
become sleek batons of ivory, gold or jade
adorning an aristocrat's table.
With their deft dance and dip,
more adroit than a fork.
Twin acrobats poised
to hoist choice morsels.

Let your elders lead, he tells me.
Never point your chopsticks at a guest.
Never spear your food like a fisherman.
Don't tap the side of your bowl like a beggar.
Keep them by the plate when you rest
or across the bowl at meal's end. But never
upright like incense burning
in an urn for the dead.

While he watches, stiff bamboo
grows nimble. One by one,
each small glassy planet arcs up
then lands with a *clink!*
The bowl gleams, empty.
Grandfather nods.

Pool

Our new L-shaped house embraced
a pool as its heart, a curving
figure eight, turquoise shimmer
mirroring turquoise clapboard.
My father's pristine pride
May through September. He'd
skim off leaves, vacuum sediment,
push the long-poled brush along the bottom
back and forth, swim laps
of breast stroke, head bobbing, arms parting
the glassy surface.

Summers I'd scamper over
searing concrete to reach the first step,
cringe against the chill, never venturing
near the shady deep end,
the dark drain's evil eye.

A church social. Laughter, splash and plunge
off the diving board we hardly used.
Barbecued hot dogs, burgers. Hawaiian punch.
My serious father smiling
the year before his death.

My mother took over,
cleaning it when she could
between long hours and locums, teaching me
to dip litmus paper for pH, pour chlorine.

Once or twice in June, the house reawakened
with school-end parties—racing kids, strewn
towels, scattered chips. Then,
hibernation. Evenings silent and dim
except for flickering reruns in the den.

The pool grew greener, murkier,
dirt swirls, dead leaves, dregs
accumulating. Rest stop for geese.
Only my mother would swim,
head bobbing, arms sweeping out
the way my father's had. Soon
even she gave up. Inside,

fissured plaster, stains
splotching carpet, counter.
Dining room heaped with plastic bags stuffed
with plastic bags, broken knick-knacks.
Overgrown shrubs shrouded the house
as each of us left. Room by room
emptied, heat turned off.
Home shrinking, porous
to elements. My mother's neurons
tangling, withering, shorting out until
the house was fully shadow.

Invisible

Tired, so tired,
held up by fraying strings,
she'd drag us through throngs
at sales. We'd shrivel,
she'd fume, yell, "Service!
I need service!"
Clerks could never
shush her.

At restaurants, overlooked
single mom with three kids, no father
to focus on, until she built beacons,
menus stacked vertically,
two or three high. After the meal,
dimes, nickels, pennies piled
atop the bill without tip.

When our old Corolla lurched, puttering
up inclines, we ducked out of sight,
flinched with each honk
from the cars zooming past.

At home, tirades. Smash and clang
in the kitchen escalating up the Richter scale
until one of us crept out to pay
penance. Better to be
invisible.

Dance

At the grade eight dance, they find you
hiding behind folded lunch tables,
seize your hands and feet, drag you
across the floor like a mop.
On the dance floor, a girl
feigns stomping on your face.

You run to the bathroom,
wipe the grime off your dress,
remove your glasses, world
become blur, gentling
to haze. If you can't see them,
they can't see you.

Cake

After school and on weekends, I'd flip through the *Five Roses and Purity Flour* cookbooks my mother bought by mailing in labels. Golden-crusted casseroles, crown roasts of pork encircled by cherry tomatoes, bowls of opalescent new potatoes speckled with parsley, glossy with butter.

I lingered over cakes—elegant stacked towers and domes, frosted and glazed, ornamented like fairy-tale hats.

Butter, chiffon, layered sponge, jelly roll, devil's food, angel's food, pound cake, genoise, coffee cakes, one-bowl quickies, cupcakes. How long to cream the butter, whether to separate the eggs, soft clouds or stiff peaks for the egg whites, when and how fast to add the sugar, what kind of sugar, how many times to alternate the dry and the liquid, whether to grease the pan. How long to bake, to cool.

Cheesecakes: New York–style, ricotta, vanilla, chocolate, chocolate marble, lemon, orange, topped with swirling mantles of whipped cream or glazed mandalas of berries. After cakes, cookies: bar, drop, thumbprint, molded, no-bake, refrigerator, rolled, sandwich. Favourite hits: Nanaimo bars, five types of brownies, peanut butter cookies with criss-crossed fork lines, chocolate chip cookies, shortbread. Then cream puffs, éclairs. For my mother's doctor colleagues, neighbours, relatives. For birthdays, Christmas, Easter. For kids who'd cluster around eager to be fed.

No idea how to make conversation, but could follow a recipe, bake my way into presence.

Piano

Weekend mornings, I was a Lazy Mary who never got up, despite how many fortissimo rounds of "Frère Jacques" my mother played. Schumann's happy farmers pranced next to marching saints, amazed with grace.

Some nights, she rolled out barrels through wild Irish roses, Chopin waltzing into Beethoven's moonlight, the piano bench her throne over kingdoms of sound. Pulse, leap, plunge of chord. Shiver and trickle of trill. Stinging pinpricks of staccato. Stalking octaves. Arpeggios cascading along the keyboard, conjured like rainbow scarves drawn from a magician's hat. All her spells honed, notes imprinting the air above the raised lid.

Vivace, allegro.
Grave, doloroso.
Moderato rarely.
Pianissimo never.

Soap

Wizened shard,
abandoned in your dish
beside other grooved and graying nubs.
Once you were whole, solid,
made for gripping. Rubbed
like a magic lamp, you melted
into your steamy work.
Clutched close in a circling, gliding
dance of lather, how you foamed,
slathered our flawed frames.
Nothing between you and us
but creamy goodness dissolving
grease, sweat, sticky sauces
of the body. Without shame,
we caressed ourselves entirely, lushly,
each toe, lobe, crevice, hollow.
We emerged purified,
radiance restored.

August Raspberries

Plucked, all those little mouths
mirror our thirst
for the season's nectar.

Deep crimson bounty enveloped
by cream clouds or suspended
in glowing realms of jam.

I woo you with the first sweet
bowl heaped with sun-warmed
nubbins under ice cream mounds.

Tangy velvet cushions
against teeth and tongue. Our mouths
royal. Last handfuls

of summer's tang hang low.
What will remain when
branches are bare?

September

Dollops of cloud
scooped up from the Pacific
garnish the heavens.

Then, spit and sprinkle, pelt
and pummel—rain's peripatetic
autumn music.

Between us, ridge and plain unfurl
under a constellation of cities.
What connects us isn't weather.

You and your brother hammer and saw
under the sun's slant gaze.
Three thousand miles away,

glancing up from a book, I listen
for those duets of metal on wood
to glimpse you through the rain.

Orange

Orange,
you are orange,
and everything orange
implies you—
sunrise, sunset, harvest moon,
crayoned spheres scribbled
low on a blue horizon or high
in a white paper sky,
rows of cones emblazoning
roadways to awaken our eyes.

Your simple five-petalled
beckoning, a fragrant
doorway. Your name,
your origin, Sanskrit
to Arabic—*naranga to naranj.*
Harkening back to ancestors
cross-bred in China—
apelsin, sinaasappel. Apple
turned orange—*pomme d'orenge.*
Or traders that bartered your splendour—
portakal, portokali.

Luminous eyes,
you peek through green
clusters of oval leaves
of trees lining the streets
of Granada, Seville, Córdoba.
Our fingers, our knives pierce
your fragrant rind and thick white pelt.
Every wedge, every wheel,
every pith-veined carpel
a showcase glistening
with your vesicles' nestling gems
ready to burst with liquid light,
condensed sun.

Stop Sign

Mighty octagon,
even from behind we know
who you are, what you say—
your command emphatic
as the shrill of a whistle,
upright wall of a hand.

A century ago, you bloomed white
and square on your stem,
prim as a raised hanky.
Then yellowed
as your sides doubled,
your stalk sprouting higher
until you loomed
over queues of cars,
transmuting the ruby
imperative of traffic lights.

Half sentry,
half grand lollipop,
you part teeming seas
of striders, shufflers, hobblers,
skippers, rollers, amblers,
the towed, the towing.
Despite squeals, screeches,
surly jolts, speed must heed
your blood-red omen.

Pockets

Dear holder and hider
of hands, let
my fingers hibernate.
You carry the sum
of my life, proof I am
who I am. Entry
to rooms or countries
in your secret
stashes. Tickets, phones,
pens, passes, matches,
linty mints, sweets
in crinkly jackets—
fingertips brush
your caches. Replete,
I pat you. Panicked,
a repeated rummage
as if you stored magic
to make the lost
reappear.

Pencil

Gnaw me.
Spin, tap, twirl me.
Delve me out
of your pockets and purses.
No obsolete coloured stick,
I'm the first
conduit: alphabetic
choreographies scratched
and scrawled in the void.
Hieroglyphic thought
turned phrase. Sharpened,
I sharpen you.
Feel free—assert, propose,
rejig, reframe. Or just
jab: your point,
mine. I can make any idea
scamper, sprint, ascend.
No need to commit.
While you whittle me
to a stub, don't let me
slip your grasp.
Even when broken inside,
ground down, like you
I still want to flow. Let me
scale mountains, curve
of cheek or hip. Trace the hover
of hummingbirds, glitter of towers.
Sketch tenderness.
Shade in time's folds.
Make me your divining rod.
I'll lead you to see
through paper into
shadow and glow. Hold me
between your teeth,
a wooden rose.

Z

Tiny zigzag on the snow
    of the page, you add sizzle
        and fizz, a spritz
      of pizzazz to words
    you visit. Electric
   eccentric, you buzz
  through fuzz
 daze
doze
snooze.
Plurals, possessives zip with your zest.
    You never fizzle. Even at zero,
      you're everyone's thunderbolt!

II

Feet

Little buds, furled
and unfurled. How you drummed
impatience against
your underwater cave,
arrived kicking away
earth and sky. We hold you
now in our palms,
rub you with our thumbs,
preparing you for life's
surfaces. Are you ready?
Thickened, coarsened,
you'll anchor wandering
through mud and sand, expanses
of floor and road. Harnessed
to haul the body's heft,
you'll tramp through
homes, towns, fields
with only a sporadic
sprint, skip, sashay,
a brief caress before
night's horizontal release.
Muffled, encased
through the day, you'll still speak—
a tap, stomp, sharp
swerve of the heel.

Milk

Milk denied, milk refused.
Milk hot and hard in the chest.
Recalcitrant milk. Hesitant milk.
Milk of the body's melting
with hidden tributaries, sudden tides.
Aching milk, urgent milk.
Milk that gushes, soaks, leaks and seeps.
Delirious milk, somnambulant milk.
Milk of pure tedium, marathon milk.
Passionate milk, appeasing milk.
Milk of solitude, dusk and twilight.
Milk languor, slumber.
Milk dreams.
Heart's milk.

Any Time from Now

When I was eight, I planned
to build a bunker in the basement closet
until the Cold War thawed.
I'd squeeze between rackets and rain boots,
stockpile toilet paper, Band-Aids, Scotch tape,
Halloween leftovers.

Decades later, ice caps warm to slush.
Polar bears amble on sidewalks.
Island nations sink like sandcastles.
Cyclones whirl us out of Oz.

"Any time from now," they say
the missiles will fly. Bellicose
threats whiz through time zones.
A million mushroom clouds
foam up in our dreams.

But today, my son went to school.
It was Pizza Day, Bowling Day,
"No Excuse" Words Spelling Day.
Front page photo of an earthquake drill:
the children smile, the premier poses,
one manicured pre-electoral hand
pointing toward a future
just beyond oblivion.

Plasticnic

Open plastic

hampers   Pop open plastic lids

of plastic clamshells   A convenient feast huddled

within   Sit on plastic chairs around plastic tables draped

with plastic   Use plastic spoons to heap food on plastic plates

Devour it with plastic forks and knives   Pour soda from plastic

bottles into plastic cups and suck it up with plastic straws while

the baby suckles on a plastic soother   Later wrap all leftovers

in new plastic   Or scrape them into old plastic   Carry

it all home in plastic   Then   take plastic out of

plastic to put on plastic shelves in the plastic

body of the fridge

Ark

In the basement, we built an ark
of hollow cardboard bricks, staggered
stacks of red, yellow, blue.
Filled the hours positioning ersatz animals
on every ledge to scrutinize an ocean
of worn beige broadloom.
At the bow, a zebra towered
over dinosaurs. A tyrannosaurus growled
its discontent behind a baboon. Port side:
herds of tiny cows and horses stared out woodenly
beside a genuine Kenyan souvenir
elephant. Starboard: jaguars, lions, no chickens,
but a duck from the upstairs tub.
At the stern, plusher creatures: sundry
teddy bears, mom and child platypuses,
black dog, red lamb, my childhood
penguin with its frayed carrot nose. We considered
the seals, sharks, dolphins, whales—
let them hitch a ride or float free to follow.
Two plastic palm trees formed the masts.
No sails. But we would save the animals
on this rainy weekend--we would
save them all.

Wolf

Of course, I admit that I have a reputation.
Connoisseur of duck sans orange.
Caribou stalker.
Cross-dressing devourer of the infirm.

Like you, I want a den of my own,
a family, to go hunting
now and then with friends,
or just sing to the moon.

Instead, I'm hyperventilating
outside houses, plunging down chimneys,
scalded in cauldrons,
swathed in sheep's clothing.

Your woodsmen clear-cut my forest,
then played target practice with the birds.
Keep pushing me to the edge
of your bucolic fantasies until   .

I'm just a distant howl
muzzled between covers
of a story I never wrote.

Forest

The trees sough and sigh as they sway,
receiving sunlight, open palmed.
Creak and moan in winter blasts.
Dawn to dusk, biophonic chorales
held within and between upheld arms—
trills, pecks, caws, thrums, hoots.

Within each trunk, clicks, pops and crackles
as tiny embolisms of air break
tension, tensile rivers coursing
in ultrasonic song up
through xylem
to bough, branch, twig,

while below the forest floor,
lacing roots entwine
in a wood wide web of questing
dendrites enmeshed in fungi
to commune with kin,
nurse saplings, nourish the ailing
or plot and warn as they record
each marauding. The forest

suspends its breath with every felled
giant. Roar of uprooted centuries,
wrenching of earthlimb from earthflesh.
Who will hear?
As the world smoulders,
let each poem be
a fallen tree's tongue.

Sparrow

I find you on the rain-soaked deck—
size of a cupped palm,
speckled russet head, cream-feathered belly,
stilled wings.

I tenderly carry your light body
to a grave beside the sage.
Small witnesses perch
on the magnolia beyond.

Dusk, drizzle,
skim of crows.

I look up to see what you saw
before you hurtled your joy
into green gleams on glass,
an imposter sky.

I look down.
One crimson drop of you,
a bright resolute eye of blood.

Holding Centre, Al-Najaf

The boy, aged four,
eyes half closed, sitting
in the red-brown dirt,
legs stretched before him,
dusty sneakers beside bare feet.
He leans against his father,
murmurs. The father listens,
clasps his son's small fingers.
His body curves over him,
a warm cocoon. Perhaps
he murmurs back—
the boy's name, a story
or lullaby. He knows
about the nightmare. We don't
know what muffled sounds
are uttered, unuttered beneath
the black hood deleting
his head and face as if burnt
through celluloid into
our eyes. Loops of barbed wire
fence man, boy
into the nightmare
that coils
into us.

Shelter

They spurn you now, your teenaged judges,
with sighs, rolled eyes, occasional grunts.
Ten years ago at the campsite near Kelowna
you settled them inside your car's sturdy frame,
your own bed, a precarious tent
propped by the doors.
Hours later, the trees conspired with night,
rain and wind pummelling the earth.
Then thunder.
One kid wriggled in after the other,
rooting limbs around you,
the three of you sheathed in the shifting skins
of a tent about to fold.
Only then could they sleep, anchored
at last to your breath and heat,
one body in the forest.

Sixteen

I wish you happy birthday, but you can't hear
through your earphones' hermetic seal.
Once upon a time you listened
when I counted forward, backward
in slivers of French, Chinese, Spanish,
sang fragments of nursery rhymes
while changing your diapers.
Later, enticed you with *Harry Potter*
out the door, down the street to school.
Lessons came sideways, glimpsed
in half smiles, chuckles, eyes wide as moons.
But it was I who learned
what not to do. Why now do I forget?

Four days from Valentine's Day, years past
frilled crayoned hearts. Should I tell you
love will not be as you expect?
How to hear words behind words
with eyes and hands. Listen
to skin, know fear or wonder
in breath. Sometimes we want
what we don't want
but don't know until the brink.
Listen. It will
weave itself into nerve and muscle,
charge every cell, endure
as shadow, echo, ripple long after
it arrives.

Postcard Tanka

geese on lake   gliding

arrowheads   sudden flurried

launch   sequenced *v*'s aimed

skyward   first   second   keeners

reluctant rearguard   rises

stranglers   drift   laggards

weary elders   or backroom

rebels revelling

honking their insurrection

before   flapping   into   form

Crow

"Canuck the Crow Voted Metro Vancouver's Unofficial Ambassador"
—CBC News

Dark star of the show,
prankster, terror, tease, bad boy,
you ride the Skytrain for free, dive-bomb letter carriers,
target cyclists' backpacks between rest stops at McDonald's.
Gas caps, cigarette packs, lighters—what's ours is yours,
at least for ten seconds (if it's shiny).
Peck on Playland cash registers like a pro,
snatch tickets at the racecourse,
plunk keys stolen months before
on a horse trainer's head. The greatest flap?
Upstage the flaming car, armed suspect, cops with guns.
Swoop down, steal the evidence, steal the scene.
Cameras rolling, give chase, knife in beak. Then soar
into notoriety—CBC, ABC, *The Guardian*,
The Washington Post, YouTube eternal, Facebook
and 116,800 followers. Your own hit movie.
No lone crow, you adopted a human pal
whose caress you'll bear, whose arm you ride with pride.
Plus nightly hangouts with a cawing choir of six thousand
at the Still Creek rookery. Then you settled down.
A wife, a nest, two kids to feed. And now to mourn
in the cycle of effort and chance. For centuries
your kind observed our foibles, became our fables.
Subject of poetic tomes. Battlefield death eater.
Hitchcock classic. Apollo's pure white messenger
burnt black for uttering truth. But you transcend
omen, symbol, metaphor. The world's your game.
Sleekly assured, you size us up with a darting glance.
A few hops, then off
to join those black streams ribboning the sky,
wings like satin fans against the dusk.

Rice

Curve upon curve,
terraces ripple a valley with sheens
of green, silver, grey, rhythmic
seams undulating as if land
were wave. Rice

for us came from Chinatown.
Rice came from stores. Rice
came in a burlap sack
hauled and tossed into the car trunk
like a sandbag, lugged upstairs
to the kitchen, sheared open
to release the cascade of white
grains into a bin under the counter.
Then scooped, triple rinsed, steamed
in our ancient rice cooker
with its rattling lid. The clicked switch
signalled dinner. Steaming
domes pillowed our bowls,
mingled with stir-fry and stew,
replenished again
and again until the cooker
was scraped to the bottom.

My father's urgent quests
through England, America,
brushing past potatoes, bread, pasta
to hunt down spartan cafés
tucked in rundown blocks.
He'd relish each mouthful
as if haunted by ancestral hungers.
Weeks without, my cravings start.
And now my son's,
as if nothing else can quell
the yearning of his cells, each
lustrous mound
a homecoming.

Peach

What lies within
your thin velvet suit?
Your hint of a tip, cleft,
voluptuous curve—
breast, derrière, cheek—
all united in promise.
Your blushing possibilities
yield to the subtlest squeeze.

Sphere of the immortals,
you've rolled through mythologies,
parched millennia—China,
India, Persia, Greece, Spain,
to the Americas—blossoming
to become munificence,
a toothsome sinking
into silken succulence, until

we reach your furrowed core,
discard the husk's
twin hemispheres, labyrinthine
as a desiccated brain,
as woody as your source,
oblivious to your sanctum
cradling life's
bitter seed.

III

Sea Star

"... the stars were blinking out."
—Ed Yong, "A Starfish-Killing Disease Is Remaking the Oceans," *The Atlantic*

A fleck of constellation stranded
in a blank expanse of shoreline.

No fragments of mollusk,
no green tendrils. No trace

of your undersea universe
beyond the ocean's undulating

border. I hover, ponder
your upturned arrival. Do I imagine

your flinch as I wake you from stasis?
You freeze, rigid.

I gingerly lift and balance
your body between twigs,

reach water's edge, flip you
right side up.

A blurred wriggle—descent
in a blink. Shallow waves wash over

impassive sand. Galaxies
of your sunflower kin dissolve

on reefs from Alaska to Mexico.
Go where the tide takes you, sea star.

What will be left?

Roll

PLASTIC PLASTIC PLASTIC INSIDIOUS PLASTIC CHOKING PLASTIC AIRBORNE PLASTIC ABS PLASTIC MELAMINE PLASTIC LDPE PLASTIC POLYAMIDE PLASTIC POLYPROPYLENE PLASTIC POLYCARBONATE PLASTIC FORMALDEHYDE PLASTIC PMMA PLASTIC PEEK PLASTIC PCDC PLASTIC PET PLASTIC POLYETHYLENE PLASTIC HDPE PLASTIC POLYSTYRENE PLASTIC BURNING PLASTIC LEACHING PLASTIC SWALLOWED PLASTIC PERVASIVE PLASTIC INVASIVE PLASTIC UBIQUITOUS PLASTIC WORLD WITHIN PLASTIC

TOSSED IN PLASTIC WRAPPED WITH PLASTIC TAPED WITH PLASTIC ENCASED IN PLASTIC WRAPPED IN PLASTIC RE-SEALED IN PLASTIC CUSHIONED IN PLASTIC AND MORE PLASTIC DISCARDED PLASTIC AND MORE PLASTIC BROKEN PLASTIC AND MORE PLASTIC SEALED WITH PLASTIC CARRIED IN PLASTIC AND MORE PLASTIC TIED WITH PLASTIC NESTLED IN PLASTIC WRAPPED IN PLASTIC INSIDE PLASTIC WITHIN PLASTIC LINED WITH PLASTIC COATED WITH PLASTIC INSIDE PLASTIC PLASTIC

POLYESTER PLASTIC POLYEPOXIDE PLASTIC POLYURETHANE PLASTIC PEI PLASTIC PVC PLASTIC THERMOPLASTIC PTFE PLASTIC DUMPED PLASTIC MUTATING PLASTIC MUTILATING PLASTIC MAIMING PLASTIC ETERNAL PLASTIC PERPETUAL PLASTIC OMNIPRESENT PLASTIC RESISTANT PLASTIC STRANGLING PLASTIC PERSISTENT PLASTIC SMOTHERING PLASTIC RELENTLESS PLASTIC PLASTIC PLASTIC PLASTIC

Ocean

Utility Pole

Once a teeming green
cosmos. 130 million of you.
Southern yellow pine,
Pacific silver fir,
lodgepole pine, Jack pine,
western red cedar,
Douglas fir.
Forest plunder
dismembered
into bald grey spines
soaked with creosote,
studding highways,
roadsides, alleys.
Column after rootless
column aligned
in a motionless
mule train criss-crossing
the continent along
infinite grids.
Telegraph, telephone,
smart meter backhaul,
video service,
internet, cable TV,
transformers, fibre
optics, equipment
enclosures, disconnect
switches, electric
meters, streetlights.
Current, pulse,
signal now sing
in your cross-arms
while you route the human.
Only woodpeckers
remember, drill you
back into tree.

Dark Mirror

i

Silent,
we sit.
Souls
flicker, sipping.
　　Mirror, mirror,
　　who loves/unloves us?
Preen, peer,
window after window after window.
A harvest of hearts
collaging
the narratives.
Exit the maze
with a few clicks.

ii

with   a few clicks
      enter   the maze
                the narratives
     collaging
          a harvest   of hearts
      window   after window   after window.
           peer   preen
who loves/unloves us?
        mirror mirror
          flicker
                    sipping
                     souls
    we sit
silent

iii

silent
    we sit

                  souls
                    flicker   sipping
Mirror, mirror
who loves/unloves us?

                  preen   peer
        window   after window   after window
              a harvest   of hearts
    collaging
      the narratives

                exit   the maze
      with   a few   clicks

iv

With a few clicks
enter the maze,
the narratives
collaging.
A harvest of hearts,
window after window after window.
Peer. Preen.
Who loves/unloves us?
      Mirror, mirror
flicker. Sipping
souls,
we sit,
silent.

Consumery

gluten free

wheat free

sugar free

wrapped in plastic

salt free   wrapped in plastic

dairy free   wrapped in plastic

MSG free   wrapped in plastic

peanut free   wrapped in plastic

fat free   wrapped in plastic

sulfate free   wrapped in plastic

cholesterol free   wrapped in plastic

lactose free   wrapped in plastic

cage free   wrapped in plastic

free range   wrapped in plastic

no artificial colours   no artificial flavours

no preservatives   no animal by-products

no high fructose corn syrup   or hormones

no antibiotics   just   wholesome

whole grain   stone ground   grass fed

fair trade   organic   all natural

freedom   wrapped in plastic

Stream by Stream

founded on the plunder of scraped rivers,
our highways, houses, our gardens of Eden,
centuries of gravel mined by the tonne

stream by stream by stream by stream

each year millions of urgent salmon
thrashed and flailed their way home,
only to reach scoured troughs

stream by stream by stream by stream

generations of eggs strewn in unsheltered shallows,
flushed away by current, or left to shrivel
on the cracked beds of stanched channels

stream by stream by stream by stream

the invisible unmourned, phantom flickers
of iridescence surge and shimmy, leaping
into absence

stream by stream by stream by stream

Prescription

An avalanche awaits you. Open
the cabinet, release a tumble
of analgesics, potions for every ailment,
complex or simple, evidence
of your failed race to function.
Cram land and ocean
with capsules, crusted bottles.
Amoxicillin, cephalexin, ciprofloxacin—
flushed down the toilet.
Dulcolax for clams, Cialis for salmon,
Robitussin for seaweed. Don't forget
Zoloft for the birds.
Spread Benadryl on the grasslands,
Celebrex on the hills.
Sorrow's past its due date. Unkilled,
pain.

Mountains

plastic
piled on
plastic piled
on plastic piled on
plastic piled on plastic
piled on plastic on plastic
piled on plastic piled on plastic
piled on plastic piled on plastic piled
on plastic piled on plastic piled on plastic
piled on plastic piled on plastic piled on plastic
on plastic piled on plastic piled on plastic piled on
on plastic piled on plastic piled on plastic piled on plastic
on plastic piled on plastic piled on plastic piled on piled on plastic
on plastic piled on plastic piled on plastic piled on piled on plastic piled
on plastic piled on plastic piled on plastic piled on piled on plastic piled on plastic
on plastic piled on plastic piled on plastic piled on piled on plastic piled on plastic on plastic
on plastic piled on plastic piled on plastic piled on piled on plastic piled on plastic on plastic on
plastic piled on plastic piled on plastic piled on piled on plastic piled on plastic on plastic on plastic

PVC

polyester

polypropylene

polystyrene polyamide

polycarbonate polyurethane

polyepoxide polyethylene terephthalate

high-density polyethylene low-density polyethylene

polyvinyl chloride polymethyl methoacrylate polyacetylene

phenol formaldehyde melamine formaldehyde urea formaldehyde

polyetheretherketone maleimide bismaleimide polyetherimide polysulfone

polyvinylidene chloride acrylonitrile butadiene styrene polytetrafluoroethylene

PC PE PVDC PET HDPE PCDC LDPE ABS HIPS PMMA PLA PEEK PEI PTFE PF MF UF

Swallow

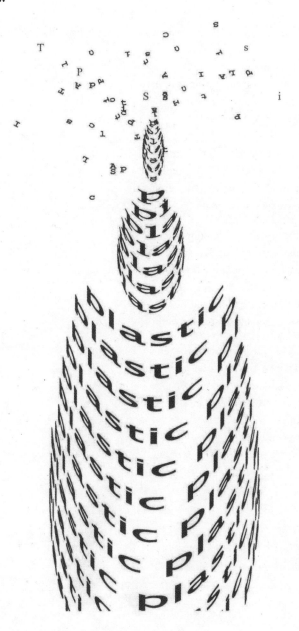

Anti-Litany

A response to Adam Zagajewski's poem "Try to Praise the Mutilated World"

I've tried to praise
those patches, shards and strands of nature
assembled into a dilute semblance
of wilderness. But all around,
waves froth and foam, slick
with jettisoned fuel from busted freighters,
slathering all in a slime of liquid night.
Every day another discarded tonne
of plastic chokes and strangles.

I cannot praise our mutilated world.
Swathes of death scraped across the ocean floor.
Poisoned lakes. Amputated forests.
Skies thick from swarming drones
and a billion corporate exhalations.
Migrants beached like discarded dolls.

What's left to praise lies on the other side
of barbed wire—those fragile, fading calls
of greenness, blueness before
they're trampled. Beauty
we remember, but
might never resuscitate.

Un/Write

Write a poem and make it disappear as you rearrange stanzas, shift

phrases from the start to the end of lines, or from end to

start, replace words and compress, distill, then distill

again, condensing description, image, intro; lop

off adjective, adverb, article, conjunction,

comma colon period whittle every-

thing down to bare essence until

ballad becomes haiku or less

phrase word syllable

riddle swallowed in

white breath a

blank wink a

naught knot

a not a

void

( )

Ode to the Short Poem

little splash   licks the rocks   carries the moon ·

Quench

Note: all words in the cup come from letters in "plastic" with no doubling. Each shift occurs with the addition or removal of a single letter and/or a reordering of the letters.

IV

Spectrum

guts: derived from the Old English *guttas* for bowels or entrails

i red

A slide show through his intestinal tunnel.
First, polyps like crimson scrawls.
Next, a fleshy pimple.
Last one, a red-jelly frog packed with maggots
blocking passage. Cancer
from the inside.

Buckle our seats for the ride
down the oncological flow chart:
biopsy reports, staging, scans, referrals.
One box leads to another
box. Unseen, *death*.

Follow the red line
that weaves through the hospital
like a vein.

ii   violet

Purple folder on the kitchen counter by the phone

>   Appointments:
>   surgeon
>   specialist
>   CT
>   ultrasound
>   pre-admission clinic
>
>   brochures
>   booklets
>   checklists
>   test results
>   instructions
>   requisitions
>   prescriptions

Compass and hub through summer and fall

iii blue

Gut surgery: the diagram for resection—
plumbing repair crossed with tailoring.
Shaved, swabbed, intubated
for visceral realignment.

gut instincts, spill one's guts, bust a gut

Four hours later, neat lines of staples,
plastic tubes to plastic sacks,
one tube connecting to a blue PCA
that ticks and clucks as if
tiny robot chickens inside
titrate hydromorphone
day and night.

right in the gut, takes guts, gutsy

Excisions hidden. Rejigged,
will the body miss
its missing pieces?

gut reaction, gut-wrenching, gutted

iv   orange

First day: Little plastic juice cups (orange, apple, grape)
                Jell-O (orange, yellow, red)
                Dishwater broths

Second day: Cream soups (carrot, broccoli, mushroom)
                Desserts (orange sherbet, vanilla ice cream, puddings)

Third day: Rice with green beans, fish
                Chicken sandwich

Then squirm. Ache. Bloat.

"Twins?" I ask. He doesn't laugh.

Towers of juice. Abandoned meals.

Ballooning traffic jam. All horns blare.

v **green**

Bizarre factory:
snaking coils of tubing suction out
internal roil of emerald seas.

Inert rows of patients "producing"
from stomach
through nose
to plastic canisters
hooked on the wall.

Filled,
emptied.

Filled,
emptied.

Filled,
emptied.

(Avoid green smoothies
for years.)

vi yellow

Push button for shot of hydromorphone from PCA
Pull on rubber-soled hospital socks
Pull on an extra hospital robe to cover backside
Disconnect NG tube
Clip Hemovac to gown
Unplug two electrical cords from wall
Drape cords on IV pole
Grip pole .
Pull up to standing
Step by step
Pass doors of the ward
A window   Pause
English Bay glitters beyond rooftops
Random choreographies below—
      traffic's wax and wane
      jaywalkers
      window shoppers
Grip pole   Push
Return

Stronger
Walk through the ward
Enter elevator
Arrive   Walk
Pass glass doors
Outside
First time in three weeks
Afternoon warm
      gold on skin
Breeze
Tears
"Must be the medication"

Tubes one by one disconnected
First shower in four weeks
Fill out forms, questionnaires
Brief on diet, pain meds
Dress in street clothes
          jeans (loose)   T-shirt (loose)
Discard wilted flowers
Give hydrangea plant to staff
Return magazines

"Good luck!" from the nurse (who changed dressings, gave injections,
adjusted the IV all month with his artificial arm and hand)

          How many patients pass through
          How many die

          Every bodily fluid
          Every kind of human being

Down elevator to parkade, then out
Late August sunlight
. Hospital behind
               block after block
                         almost
                              home
          free

Photograph

One pupil clouded powder blue
behind her spectacles, blue
as sky beyond drawn curtains.

Pearl necklace looped around her frail fingers,
eyebrows knit together, lips turn inward.
She refuses the camera's stare.

On her wrist, her watch,
its face also turned away. No need
to look at time. Three decades

between you. High foreheads,
left-parted hair, delicate chins.
You are your mother's daughter, summer

in a tilting winter house,
slanting shelves with ornamental pitchers,
framed photos pitched perilously

as if slowly sliding to a fall.
You hold her close, knowing.

Fortune

After the diagnosis, omens everywhere.
Ladders, sidewalk cracks, splintered mirrors.

At meal's end, no future
in an empty cookie's augury.

        Fortune holds her tongue.

Tumour excised. Relief
ebbs: rogue cells lurk in a sentinel node.

        Luck slips in, slips out.
        Answers lie elsewhere.

Chemo haze, singed cells.
Who can love you now?

        Value the intangible.
        In lack find plenitude.

Scorched, you return.

        Fear not the void.
        Eat absence.

Cusp

Your mother's body, papery and hollow.
Infected limbs darkening
under pale sheets. The distance
she has travelled
away from you. Everyone
hovers without wings.

She cannot know this, reduced to
pain, no pain.

The certainties to come:
black clothes, burial plot,
names to phone, house to empty,
drawer by brimming drawer.

Upstream

Highways of still-spawning pinks,
ocean to stream. Slick
black bodies rise half out
of the shallows, slide back,
flick past. Stew of fish shreds, milt,
dams of waylaid, bloated chum
clotted with maggots.
Beneath a submerged spruce,
a teeming cauldron, hundreds
of salmon churning and swirling,
the way we churn, swirl, collide,
striving and failing to love
or hold love or even arrive—
our boots slipping against shifting pebbles,
air redolent of rot and bear scat
as we clamber upstream.

Vocation

You were supposed to be a doctor
like your white-coated parents,
superheroes with stethoscopes
on a mission to heal across continents.

You can't stop death
with elegy or rant. Words clot
in fingers into contortions of gibberish.
Medicine for no one.

Yet your scrutiny won't cease--
shudder of a sleeping lover,
a child's panting deepening into peace,
flicker of your mother's eyelids.
Gulp, gasp, sob, shiver, quake.
Symptom becomes symbol. The heart,
defective clock, plugged pump,
or more? Slice into the past and delve
for what festers. Suture with words
life's ragged fissures.
The poem remains,
a small silvery trail.

Matches

After José Guerrero's painting *Intervalos negros*

On an airplane, high above cities,
between time zones,
a book of matches lit
José Guerrero's magnifying gaze.
Cradled in his palm, incendiary

      columns thrusting up
      into white stone arches

      or a barricade of soldiers,
      white helmets like skulls

      or lightless shafts ascending
      to explosions, implosions

On an airplane, high above cities,
between time zones,
a book of matches. He sees
night seared open,
cradled in his palm, incendiary.

The Concert

After the painting *The Concert* by Johannes Vermeer

Angled light on her white collar and bodice, she sings, a hand caressing a rising phrase from the slip of music she holds above the curve of her pregnant belly.

Intent at her keyboard, face in shadow, the harpsichordist's head bends as if in prayer. Follow the brushstrokes of yellow ribbon in her hair down to the golden puff of sleeve, her arms distilling sunlight into chord.

And if it weren't for the red chair at the centre, the white glimpse of his cuff, you'd almost miss the lute player, his head and broad shoulders a dark hill against a bright landscape on the harpsichord's open lid, its tamed harmony of foliage and summer sky. Absorbed, he blends into music, his back to us, audience irrelevant.

Lemon

After *Points of Lemon*, a woodblock print by
Masato Arikushi of the painting by Mary Pratt

The lemon surrenders itself,
wedges of light ignited
by late afternoon sun, burnishing
the silver boat of its saucer that floats
atop the table's inky glimmer.
Translucent layers of shadow
fall like spires, ghost
leaves from a forgotten grove.
At the centre, incandescence.

Ghazal for Gestating Poems

Tantalized by the promise of nascent poems?
How the world rustles when we listen for poems!

A mother's old purse, fresh baked bread, petrichor.
Smoke and clover waft around us, scents of poems.

Metaphors crystallized during sleep dissipate
on waking, lost in the depths, those lucent poems.

Try to conjure spells to trace paths to their magic.
Each trail fades, dead ended—recalcitrant poems.

Mine a life for incident—love, betrayal, death.
But everything's cliché. Damned transparent poems!

Species vanish, refugees thirst, autocrats rise.
Can we dismantle walls with eloquent poems?

Your enjambments confuse, the last stanza eludes.
They stalk your subconscious, somnambulant poems.

No one cares or buys. They want celebrity prose.
Why bother writing these obsolescent poems?

Poet, dive deeper, probe, caress, meander, leap.
Windows will open. Stay bent over your poems.

Potato

On the table's altar,
roast meats and ornate sweets
might claim the limelight.
But for you we labour
through the necessary ablutions,
scraping skin, gouging out
imperfection to reveal
your pearly flesh.
Stalwart one, you cushion
against famine's edge
with the reprise of storied feasts,
steaming clouds
crowned with molten gold.

One afternoon, I plunged
my hands in dirt, seeking
your lumps of rosy, tawny treasure.
Soul of the soil, how you gleamed
in the damp loam as if gods
had transformed stones to sate
the hungers of the world.
Your many eyes questing in darkness
for moisture, mineral, sun
gazed up at me.

Lost Stream

Forgotten one, you remember what you were:
mossy banks, fringes of fern, rivulets, riffles,
cool passage for salmon. On a map
of old streams spilling out to the strait
you were one of hundreds
of capillaries threading through earth
muscled with rock, lavished with forest.
Then the city donned concrete
masks, civilized grids. Smothered
into park, you were culverted, diverted, yoked,
locked into pipes while we romped above.
But you refuse to be choked
under clear-cut, brush cut tracts. Playing fields
soak back into marsh. Bog rises through playground.
One by one, oaks topple in sodden soil,
upended roots like tangled claws.
Submerged roads around you
ripple in wind. Water above seeks
water below. Deep underground,
you gurgle, chortle, ready to rise.

NOTES TO POEMS

Page 5: The opening epigraph by Pablo Neruda was quoted by Ilan Stavans in his introduction to *The Poetry of Pablo Neruda* (New York: Farrar, Straus and Giroux, 2003), xxxiii.

Page 12, "Vision": Drusen are yellow extracellular deposits made of lipids (a fatty protein) that accumulate under the retina. They can be an early sign of age-related macular degeneration (AMD) when they become larger and more numerous in the macula.

Page 16, "Pool": A longer, non-fiction narrative was published in *The Summer Book*, edited by Mona Fertig (Salt Spring Island: Mother Tongue Publishing, 2017), 140-149.

Page 35, "Any Time from Now": The title of this poem was taken from a quote by South Korea's Foreign Minister about the threat of nuclear attack from North Korea. Choe Sang-Hun, "U.S. and South Korea Put Forces on Alert for Missile Test by North," *The New York Times*, April 10, 2013, https://www.nytimes.com/2013/04/11/world/asia/north-korea-missile.html.

Page 36, "Plasticnic": This poem is the basis of an animated video poem produced in collaboration with animator Tisha Deb Pillai and sound designer Tinjun Niu in 2018, https://vimeo.com/267531514.

Page 39, "Forest": This poem was inspired by a line in *The Lorax* by Dr. Seuss (New York: Random House, 1971). The "wood wide web" is a wonderful term referred to by forester Peter Wohlleben who refers to the research of Dr. Suzanne Simard of UBC in his book *The Hidden Life of Trees* (Vancouver: Greystone Books, 2016) 10-11.

Page 40, "Sparrow": Environment Canada ranked window collisions as the second highest direct human cause of bird deaths in Canada. Ninety percent of these collisions are with windows in individual houses, about 9 percent from low-rise buildings and under 1 percent from high-rises and skyscrapers. An estimated twenty-five million birds are killed in collisions with buildings across Canada yearly. "Cats and Collisions: Windows," *Nature Canada*, November 1, 2017.

Page 41, "Holding Centre, Al-Najaf": This poem is based on the World Press Photo of the Year in 2004, taken by Jean-Marc Bouju on March 31, 2003, https://www.worldpressphoto.org/collection/photo/2004/world-press-photo-year/jean-marc-bouju.

Page 45, "Crow": This poem is about Canuck, East Vancouver's celebrity crow who was named Metro Vancouver's Unofficial Ambassador after receiving more than 300,000 votes in a CBC poll. "Shock and Caw: Canuck the Crow Voted Metro Vancouver's Unofficial Ambassador," CBC News, August 17, 2018, https://www.cbc.ca/news/canada/british-columbia/canuck-the-crow-voted-vancouver-s-unofficial-ambassador-1.4788909.

Page 51, "Sea Star": "Wherever they looked, they saw dead and dying sea stars. Some had disintegrated into white mush. Others were still alive, their body riddled with sores and their arms twisting at grotesque angles. Yet others seemed to be pulling themselves apart." Quoted from "A Starfish-Killing Disease Is Remaking the Oceans" by Ed Yong in *The Atlantic*, January 30, 2019, https://www.theatlantic.com/science/archive/2019/01/starfish-killing-disease-remaking-oceans/581632/.

Scientists began noticing in 2013 that populations of sea stars, especially sunflower sea stars, were declining between 80 and 100 percent in deep and shallow waters, from Alaska and British Columbia to California and Mexico. An increase in temperature makes the sea stars more susceptible to a disease that is already present. More than twenty species of sea stars have been affected by this wasting disease, including the ochre and sunflower sea stars. "Spread of 'Zombie' Disease Killing Off Starfish Linked to Rising Ocean Temperatures," CBC, January 19, 2019, https://www.cbc.ca/radio/asithappens/as-it-happens-thursday-edition-1.5000687/spread-of-zombie-disease-killing-off-starfish-linked-to-rising-ocean-temperatures-1.5000694; Lisa Johnson, "Sea Star Wasting Disease Among Worst Wildlife Die-offs Say Scientists," CBC, January 21, 2016), https://www.cbc.ca/news/canada/british-columbia/sea-star-wasting-die-off-1.3414607.

Pages 52–53, "Roll" and "Ocean": These two poems are the basis of another animated video poem entitled "Plasticpoems," produced in collaboration with animator Nhat Truong and sound designer Tinjun Niu in 2019, https://fionalam.net/filmvideo/.

Page 54, "Utility Pole": Statistics and information about utility poles: https://woodpoles.org/WhyWoodPoles/HowPolesAreMade.aspx. The word *utility* reminded me of a quote by John Muir, founder of the Sierra Club: "A numerous class of men are painfully astonished whenever they find anything, living or dead, in all God's universe, which they cannot eat or render in some way what they call useful to themselves." John Muir, *A Thousand-Mile Walk to the Gulf* (New York: Houghton Mifflin, 1916), https://vault.sierraclub.org/john_muir_exhibit/writings/mans_place_in_the_universe.aspx.

Page 55, "Dark Mirror": This poem is a palindrome. The inversion and repetition of that form has been used here to depict addictions to social media, online dating and porn.

Page 60, "Stream by Stream": "[W]e're losing them, losing the fish and habitat, stream by stream by stream." Frank Kwak quoted in Tyee Bridge's "Gravel Battle in the Fraser River," *BC Business*, July 7, 2010.

Page 64, "Anti-Litany": A response to Adam Zagajewski, "Try to Praise the Mutilated World" in *Without End: New and Selected Poems* (New York: Farrar, Straus & Giroux, 2002) 60.

Page 65, "Un/Write" is a response to a line in the poem "Backwards" by Warsan Shire at https://www.poetryfoundation.org/poems/90734/backwards.

Page 71, "Spectrum": PCA stands for patient-controlled analgesia. A Hemovac is a type of drain for internal fluids. A non-fiction narrative version of this piece was published in Full Grown People, November 16, 2017. http://fullgrownpeople.com/2017/11/16/spectrum/.

Page 84, "The Concert": This poem is based on an oil painting by Johannes Vermeer that was stolen from Boston's Isabella Stewart Gardner Museum in 1990 and never recovered.

DEDICATIONS

"Libation" is dedicated to Shannon Cowan and Apple Lane Orchards, which has an orchard of heritage apple trees on Denman Island.

"Crow" is dedicated to Canuck, East Van's favourite crow.

"Forest" is dedicated to Theodor Seuss Geisel also known as Dr. Seuss.

"Ocean" is dedicated to Captain Charles Moore who discovered the Great Pacific Garbage Patch gyre in 1997.

"Spectrum" is dedicated to my partner, Ted.

"Photograph" is dedicated to Susan Olding.

"Fortune" is dedicated to Barbara Henn-Pander.

"Potato" is dedicated to Deborah Campbell.

"Lost Stream" is dedicated to Rita Wong and streamkeepers all over the world who work tirelessly to daylight lost streams and preserve existing ones.

ACKNOWLEDGEMENTS

Previous versions of these poems have appeared in the following literary magazines and anthologies:

"Photograph" in *The Antigonish Review*;

"Sea Star" and "Ode to a Crow" (now "Crow") in *Cascadia Magazine*;

"Vocation" (formerly published as "Doctor") in *Communion*;

"Lemon" in *Eclectica*;

"The Concert" in *The Ekphrastic Review*;

"Postcard Tanka" in *EVENT*;

"Swallow" in *filling station*;

"Consumery" and "Mountains" in *The Goose*;

"Wolf" in *Grain*;

"Ode to a Crow" (now "Crow") in *Migration Songs* (a chapbook edited by Stephen Collis, Lorna Crozier and Kurt Trzcinski, prepared for the twenty-seventh International Ornithological Congress, 2018);

"Juice" (now "Libation"), "Chopsticks" (formerly published as "Test"), "Ode to the Plate" (now "Plate"), "Ode to the Peach" (now "Peach"), and "Ode to the Potato" (now "Potato") in *The New Quarterly*;

"Roll" and "Cupped" (now "Quench") in *oratorealis*;

"Ocean" and "Plasticnic" in *RAUM*;

"Anti-Litany" in the anthology *Refugium: Poems for the Pacific*, edited by Yvonne Blomer (Halfmoon Bay: Caitlin Press, 2017);

"Milk" (formerly "Ode to Milk"), "Pool", "Invisible" and "Dance" in *Ricepaper Magazine*;

"Shelter" in *Room* magazine and in the anthology *Making Room: Forty Years of Room Magazine*, edited by Meghan Bell (Halfmoon Bay: Caitlin Press, 2017).

Many thanks to Anne Simpson, poetry midwife, for her invaluable experience, insights, attentive editing and expert eye, and to Susan Olding for our creative exchanges during dark days when writing seemed either futile or impossible. Gratitude to those generous individuals who inspired the generation of new poems and/or gave feedback on some of them, including Evelyn Lau, the Power of Six collective (Kate Braid, Pam Galloway, Heidi Greco, Tana Runyan, Leslie Timmins), Loretta Seto, Jane Silcott, Miranda Pearson, Betsy Warland, Analee Weinberger and my son Robbie. The encouragement of dear, long-time friends and my partner Ted replenished me throughout the writing and editing process.

My siblings Bruce Lam and Shona Lam provided essential logistical assistance. Shannon Cowan patiently taught me how to use WordArt on my ancient refurbished laptop, which I used to fashion the plasticpoems. H. Kristen Campbell helped with the formatting of the spiral poem. Tisha Deb Pillai, Nhat Truong and Tinjun Niu were my creative collaborators on the animated video poem versions of the plasticpoems from this collection.

Thank you to my poetry students, whose passion for poetry always reignites my own. My appreciation to Christa Lynn, Dr. Gary Ryder and Barbara Weston for their years of support.

Small and independent presses are the backbone of Canadian literature: my deep gratitude to Vici Johnstone, Holly Vestad, Monica Miller, and Sarah Corsie at Caitlin Press.

ABOUT THE AUTHOR

Fiona Tinwei Lam has authored two poetry books and a children's book. She edited *The Bright Well: Contemporary Canadian Poems on Facing Cancer* (Leaf Press, 2011) and co-edited *Love Me True: Writers Reflect on the Ins, Outs, Ups & Downs of Marriage* with Jane Silcott (Caitlin Press, 2018). She has won *The New Quarterly*'s Nick Blatchford Occasional Verse Contest and was a finalist for the City of Vancouver Book Award. Her work appears in over thirty anthologies, including *The Best of the Best Canadian Poetry in English: The Tenth Anniversary Edition* and *Forcefield: 77 Women Poets of BC.* Her poetry videos have screened at festivals locally and internationally. She teaches at Simon Fraser University's Continuing Studies. *Odes & Laments* is her third collection of poetry. www.fionalam.net